I0167521

Amazing Animal Migration

This course was written by
Naturally Curious Expert
Kira Freed

Kira used to be an archaeozoologist. Now she writes science materials for children. She is curious about all the different forms of life in our world.

Printed by CreateSpace

ISBN 978-1-942403-12-8

www.benaturallycurious.com

Many activities in this book make use of printed materials. If you prefer not to cut them directly from this book, please visit the URL listed below and enter the code for a supplemental PDF containing all printable materials.

URL: www.benaturallycurious.com/migrations-printables/

password: **path**

Table of Contents

Required materials: Scissors, glue, game markers (coins, beans, or markers from a different game), one die (or spinner from a different game), crayons (or markers or colored pencils), yarn or string, bath towel (one for each child), timer, electric fan

The Migration Awards

Welcome, everyone, to the second annual Migration Awards. I'm Pedro Penguin, your host for the evening. Tonight we're here to honor a group of courageous animals from around the world. These animals are all champion migrants—animals that migrate.

For those of you who aren't familiar with migration, let me explain. MIGRATION is a pattern of movement from one place to another that a type of animal follows, usually several times a year. The animals we're honoring tonight travel amazing distances and often endure unbelievable hardships when they migrate. We'll hear some of their stories in a little while.

But first, I'd like to introduce two friends of mine who will be explaining a little more about migration. The first one will share with you a bit about why animals might migrate. I'd like to introduce Dani Dragonfly.

"Hello, everyone. Animals migrate for many different reasons, and we don't really understand all of them. But here are some reasons we know about."

Migration is a movement pattern followed by an animal, usually more than once a year.

WHY ANIMALS MIGRATE

FOOD

Many animals migrate to find food. They may leave an area in winter or during a dry season, when plant food isn't available. For example, zebras, gazelles, and wildebeests migrate to areas where rain falls so they can find food.

TEMPERATURE

Animals may also migrate to escape harsh temperatures. You may have heard about some types of birds flying south for the winter. They're spending the winter in a warmer place.

SHELTER

Some animals migrate to find a safe SHELTER. For example, little brown bats HIBERNATE, or sleep, all winter. They migrate to get to their winter cave roosts.

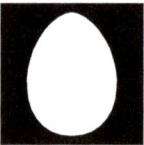

> **S**helter is any place that offers protection from bad weather or danger.

LAY EGGS/RAISE YOUNG

Some animals migrate to places where they can lay eggs or raise their young. Salmon return to the river or stream where they hatched in order to lay eggs. Emperor penguins go to nesting sites in Antarctica to protect their eggs and care for their young.

> **W**hen animals *hibernate*, they go into a state of rest or deep sleep, often during winter.

ESCAPE PREDATORS

Animals may also migrate to escape PREDATORS. For example, a fish called the common roach migrates from lakes to small streams to escape cormorants—birds that are known to eat them.

> **P**redators are animals that hunt and eat other animals for food.

As you read the animal stories on the next pages, pay attention to why each type of animal migrates. (There may be more than one reason!) Then cut out the icons on page 15 and glue the correct one(s) in the box(es) next to each animal's story.

Thanks very much, Dani. Now I'd like to introduce Christopher Crab, who will answer a very interesting question: How do animals know where they're going when they migrate?

"Greetings, everyone. It's a pleasure to be here. Animals have many different ways of knowing where they're going."

HOW ANIMALS KNOW WHERE THEY'RE GOING

LANDMARKS
Many animals navigate by sight using familiar LANDMARKS. For example, elephants use rivers and mountains. They remember those landmarks over many years.

Landmarks are easily seen objects on land that can help an animal find its way.

SUN
Many types of birds use the position of sun to know which direction to go. That's a pretty advanced ability since sun's position in the sky changes throughout the day.

MOON AND STARS
Birds that migrate at night use the moon and stars to know where they're going. They may fly at night for many reasons. It's cooler at night, and the air is usually calmer and less dry. Also, the birds may be safer from predators at night.

MAGNETIC FIELD
Some animals know where to go because they use Earth's MAGNETIC FIELD. Some migrating birds and fish have a magnetic mineral called *magnetite* in their nasal cavities, which works like a built-in compass. It's quite possible that bats and sea turtles do, too.

Earth's *magnetic field* is an area around Earth where there is a magnetic force, which pushes and pulls certain metals.

SUNRISE/SUNSET
Detecting certain kinds of light at sunrise and sunset helps some animals find their way.

SMELL
Some migrating animals use their sense of smell to know where to go. For example, they smell their home river, the ocean, or the scent of a certain type of tree in a forest they are looking for.

Thank you, Christopher—that's fascinating information. And now I want to spend a moment honoring *all* animals that migrate for their incredible courage. Many of them don't eat at all on their long trips, and they aren't even sure that food will be waiting for them when they arrive. Also, they face many difficult situations on their journeys. These include predators, human hunters, pollution, power lines, changing land, blocked rivers, and artificial light, which can confuse them.

Scientists are working to discover more about the trips that migrating animals take and how to help them. People in many locations help scientists by reporting their SIGHTINGS. By participating in CITIZEN SCIENCE projects, they help scientists gather information for their research.

Well, that concludes the educational part of our evening. So without further delay, it's time to present the Migration Awards. Each winner will receive this beautiful award.

Sightings are acts of seeing something, especially something unusual, for a short period of time.

Citizen science projects involve the general public collecting and studying information about the natural world, usually as part of a project run by scientists.

What are you CURIOUS about?

Our first category is **Longest Mammal Migration**. We have a tie in this category between two cousins. The winners are the humpback whale and gray whale! Let's learn about each whale's migration.

HUMPBACK WHALE

Humpback whales migrate each year from their summer FEEDING GROUNDS to their winter BREEDING GROUNDS. In summer, they feed on tiny ocean animals near the North and South Poles. In winter, they travel toward the equator so they can mate, give birth, and care for their calves in warmer waters. They may travel 5,157 miles (8,300 km) or more each way when they migrate.

Why do humpback whales migrate?

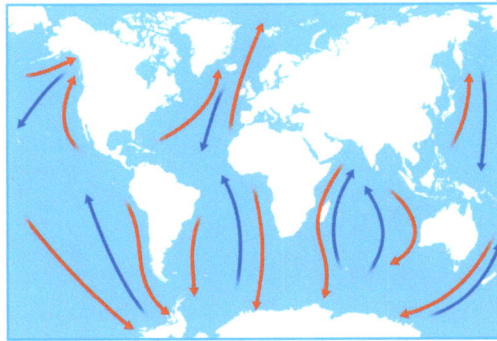

Feeding grounds are natural areas where a group of animals go to look for food and eat it.

Breeding grounds are natural areas where a group of animals regularly go to mate, lay eggs or give birth, and raise their young.

GRAY WHALE

Gray whales migrate for the same reason as their cousins, the humpbacks. They travel between summer feeding grounds and winter breeding grounds. Their feeding grounds are in the seas to the west of Alaska. They migrate to lagoons in Baja California, Mexico, to mate and give birth. Gray whales may cover 5,000 miles (8,000 km) or more each way.

Why do gray whales migrate?

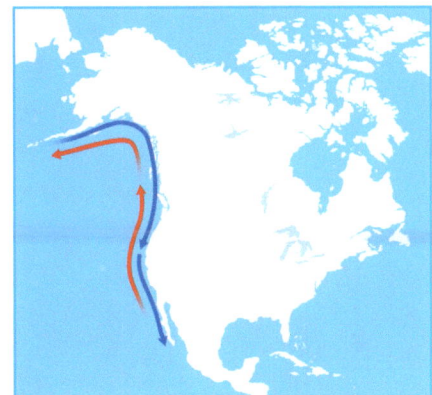

Now it's time to honor another mammal—one that's much smaller. This award is for the **Largest Mammal Migration**, and the winner is … the straw-colored fruit bat!

STRAW-COLORED FRUIT BAT

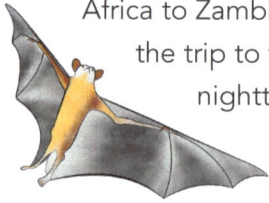 Every November and December, straw-colored fruit bats—up to eight million of them!—migrate from many parts of tropical Africa to Zambia, which is in central Africa. They make the trip to feast on their favorite fruit at night. If a nighttime predator tries to attack them, a large group of bats work together to chase it away.

For a long time, no one knew where these bats lived the rest of the year. However, a scientist fitted four of the bats with special collars and followed their movements on a map. The bats she tracked traveled 621 miles (1,000 km) in a single month after leaving. And one bat tracked earlier by a different scientist traveled 1,180 miles (1,900 km) in a period of six months. No one knows if that bat traveled farther before turning around. Even if it didn't, a round trip would have been at least 2,360 miles (3,800 km). That's a *very* long trip for a bat!

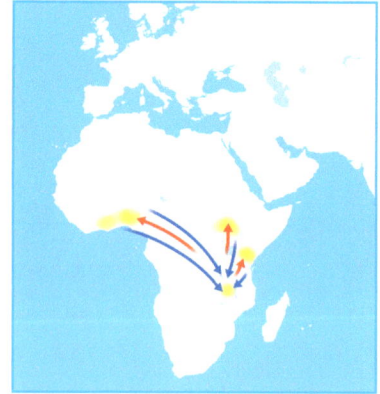

Why do straw-colored fruit bats migrate?

Now we're going to turn to a completely different group of animals. These animals prove that migrating animals come in all shapes and sizes. You might not think that really small animals are strong enough to migrate, but that's not true at all. This category is **Longest Insect Migration**, and the winner is … the globe skimmer dragonfly!

GLOBE SKIMMER

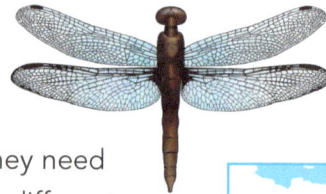

Globe skimmers are dragonflies that make a very long trip every year. They fly from southern India to eastern and southern Africa. Because they need fresh water to breed, they follow the rains in the different places. Wind currents help them make the long trip. Their flight each way can be as long as 5,600 miles (9,000 km).

Why do globe skimmers migrate?

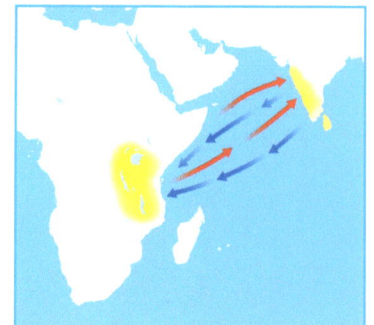

We also have an honorable mention in this category. Congratulations to the monarch butterfly!

MONARCH BUTTERFLY

Most monarch butterflies live in parts of North America that have harsh winters. For this reason, monarchs migrate south to places in Mexico and California with mild winters. They are the only insects that make such a long trip every year to find warmth.

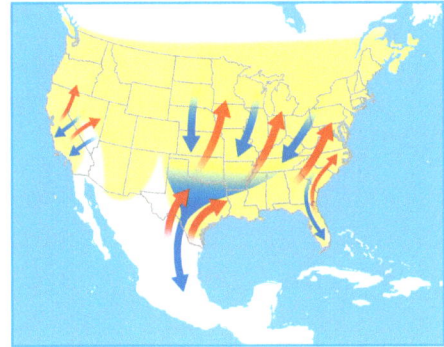

Monarchs migrate for another reason, too. Milkweed plants, which are the only food of monarch caterpillars, only grow in the colder locations. So monarchs make the long trip south for warmth and north again for food for their caterpillars.

Monarchs live on both sides of the Rocky Mountains. The ones east of the Rockies migrate to oyamel fir trees in Mexico. The monarchs west of the Rockies migrate to eucalyptus trees in the area around Pacific Grove, California. In both locations, the monarchs hibernate, or sleep, all winter. Their trip each way can be as long as 3,100 miles (5,000 km).

Why do monarch butterflies migrate?

Our next award is for the **Longest Reptile Migration**. Congratulations to our winner … the leatherback sea turtle!

*T*ropical areas usually have hot, humid weather.

*T*emperate areas usually have mild temperatures.

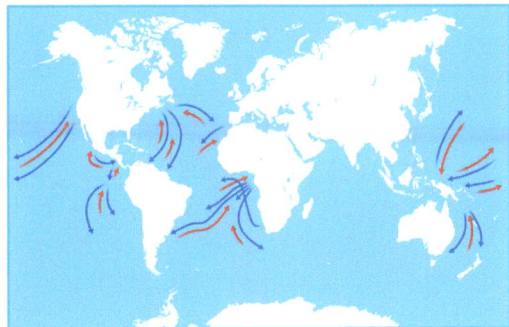

LEATHERBACK SEA TURTLE

Leatherback sea turtles live throughout the Atlantic, Pacific, and Indian Oceans. They migrate between TROPICAL breeding grounds and many different feeding grounds in tropical and TEMPERATE waters. They also swim long distances to return to the beaches where they hatched in order to mate and lay eggs. They travel about 3,700 miles (6,000 kilometers) each way.

Why do leatherback sea turtles migrate?

The next award is for the **Longest Water Migration**. Congratulations to …
the Atlantic bluefin tuna!

ATLANTIC BLUEFIN TUNA

Atlantic bluefin tuna are large, fast fish
that are among the most migratory of
all fish. Two separate groups of Atlantic
bluefins feed together in the Atlantic Ocean.
However, they migrate thousands of miles in opposite directions to
reach their SPAWNING GROUNDS—the place where they lay
eggs. One group swims to the Gulf of Mexico and the other to the
Mediterranean Sea. Although
Atlantic bluefins follow different
routes, they travel over 4,800
miles (7,700 km) each way.

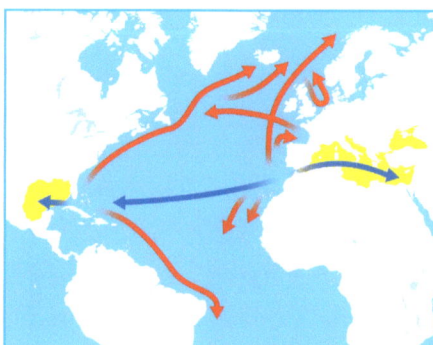

**Why do
Atlantic bluefin
tuna migrate?**

Spawning grounds
are natural areas where
fish or certain other
animals go to lay their
eggs in water.

Now we want to honor a very special migrating animal that is receiving two awards—
one for **Smallest Migrating Animal** and the other for **Most Unusual Migration**.
Congratulations to … zooplankton!

ZOOPLANKTON

Zooplankton are tiny non-swimming, drifting
creatures in the ocean that eat other creatures. They
have an unusual migration pattern—they migrate up
and down! They move to deep water each morning
and rise at sunset. Zooplankton eat tiny ocean plants
that need sunlight, which means they need to be
near the surface of the ocean. But feeding there is
dangerous to zooplankton because that's also
where the predators are. So zooplankton come
to the surface to feed as the sun is going down.
During the day, they drop to deeper levels to
avoid being eaten. Smart zooplankton!

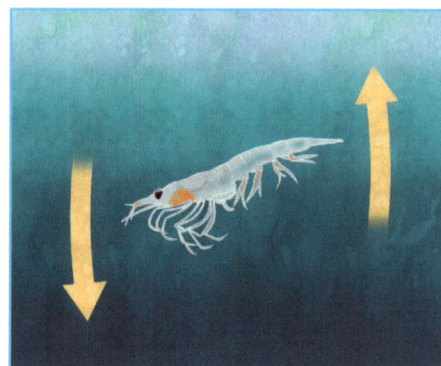

**Why do
zooplankton
migrate?**

Our next category of migration is for high altitude—in other words, how high up in the air the animal travels. The winner of the **Highest Migration** is the bar-headed goose. Congratulations to this amazing bird!

BAR-HEADED GOOSE

The bar-headed goose is one of the highest flyers in the bird world and the highest migrating bird. It breeds near mountain lakes in Central Asia and spends winters in South Asia, where it mainly feeds on human food crops. To get from one region to the other, this goose must fly over the Himalaya Mountains, where most of Earth's highest peaks are found. Bar-headed geese have flown at least as high as 8,481 m (27,825 ft) and possibly higher, though most don't fly quite that high. Like other geese, bar-headed geese fly in a V-formation to conserve energy.

Why do bar-headed geese migrate?

This year, we have a new category, which is the **Smallest Bird Migrant**. And the winner is … the ruby-throated hummingbird!

RUBY-THROATED HUMMINGBIRD

Ruby-throated hummingbirds live in North America during the warmer seasons. However, they migrate to Central America for food in winter. People think of hummingbirds as living on nectar (the juice of flowers), but they just drink nectar for energy. Their main food is insects and spiders, which are hard to find during North America's cold winters, so they fly south. These tiny birds don't travel in flocks—they make the trip alone. They fly nonstop up to 525 miles (845 km) across the Gulf of Mexico, and that's just one part of their trip! They may fly another 1,000 miles (1,600 km) to get where they're going in Central America. And the ones that nest in Canada may have already flown 1,000 miles (1,600 km) to get to the Gulf of Mexico.

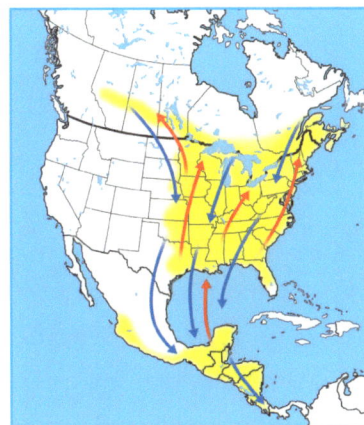

Why do ruby-throated hummingbirds migrate?

We have another new category this year—**Most Colorful Migration**. Migrating animals come in many different colors. However, if you want to see a colorful group of animals on the move, none is more colorful than … the Christmas Island red crab! Congratulations!

CHRISTMAS ISLAND RED CRAB

Every fall on Australia's Christmas Island, huge numbers of red crabs march from the forest to the coast to breed and release their eggs into the ocean. As they move to the coast, they look like a moving carpet of red. So many crabs are on the move—fifty million or more!—that roads must often be closed.

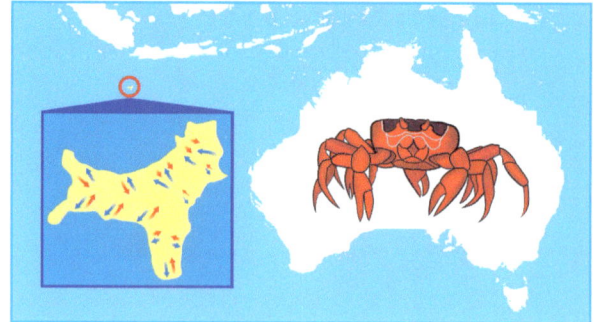

Why do Christmas Island red crabs migrate?

And now for our final award. This award is for the **Longest Migration**—of any type and size of animal anywhere in the world. Let's all give a hearty round of applause for … the arctic tern!

ARCTIC TERN

The arctic tern is a seabird that migrates between the North and South Poles to find food and a warm place to live. It spends summers near the North Pole. Before fall comes, it takes off for the South Pole and stays there for up to five months. Then it returns to the North Pole the next spring. It flies a whopping 44,000 miles (71,000 km) each year!

Why do arctic terns migrate?

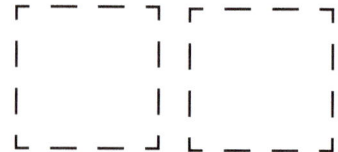

Summer in the Northern Hemisphere is June through August. In the Southern Hemisphere, summer is December through February. The arctic tern migrates from one summer to the other summer and back again. Summers have more sunlight than any other time of year. Scientists think the arctic tern sees more daylight than any other animal in the world!

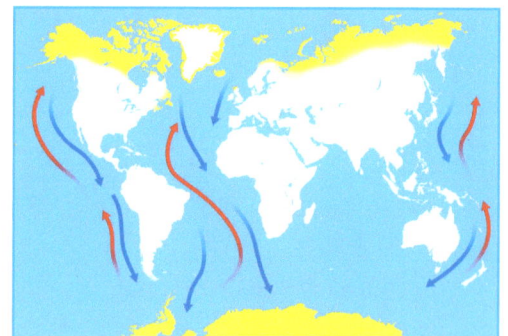

Let's give another hearty round of applause to all our winners—and to all migrating animals everywhere. You're amazing, and you inspire us all!

Thanks, everyone, for joining us for this awards show. Let's all take good care of our planet so we all continue to have good food, safe shelters, and healthy places to live and play. Goodnight!

FOOD

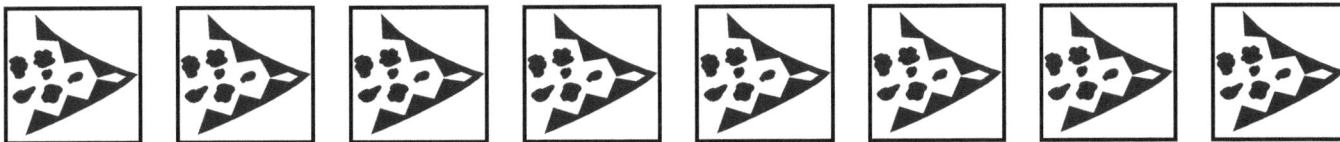

TEMPERATURE

SHELTER

LAY EGGS/RAISE YOUNG

ESCAPE PREDATORS

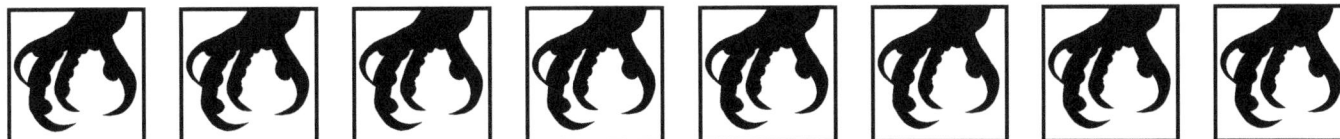

ANSWER KEY:

Humpback whale: food and raise young; Gray whale: food and raise young; Straw-colored fruit bat: food; Globe skimmer: lay eggs; Monarch butterfly: food and escape harsh temperatures; Leatherback sea turtle: food and lay eggs; Atlantic bluefin tuna: lay eggs; Zooplankton: escape predators and food; Bar-headed goose: food and lay eggs; Ruby-throated hummingbird: food; Christmas Island red crab: lay eggs; Arctic tern: food and escape harsh temperatures

You're a Salmon!

ACTIVITY 1

Did you ever hear about how Pacific salmon migrate? These fish hatch in fresh water and live part of their lives there. Then they migrate to the ocean to live in salt water! (Not many animals can live in both fresh water and salt water.) When the salmon are adults, they swim back to the exact same place where they hatched so they can spawn, or lay their eggs. The trip back to their home river, lake, or stream is very hard. Salmon face many challenges during their journey, and many of them don't survive. The urge to reproduce, or make more of their kind, pushes them to make this difficult trip.

As salmon migrate to the ocean and back, they have to deal with many problems, including predators such as sea lions, eagles, and bears. Another problem is fishing nets, which catch many of the salmon. Also, the water itself may be a problem. Salmon need cool, clean water to be healthy. They have a tough time if a factory puts chemicals or hot water into a stream. Problems can also be caused by water levels that are too low or changes caused by flooding.

Also, a dam may block the waterway back to their birthplace. Luckily, some dams have fish ladders next to them. A fish ladder is a group of low steps with water that salmon can swim up. It's a great invention for the salmon that find one, but not all of these fish do. Salmon are important to the balance of nature. Many people are studying salmon and trying to figure out how to help them stay alive.

Read about the life cycle of a Pacific salmon on the next page. Then get ready—you're about to become a Pacific salmon! Follow the path on the game board from where you hatch all the way to the ocean and back again. The first player to safely return to your spawning ground wins the game!

You're a Salmon!

(continued)

LIFE CYCLE OF A PACIFIC SALMON

A female Pacific salmon builds a nest—called a *redd*—in gravel at the bottom of a freshwater stream, river, or lake. She lays her eggs in the nest and then covers them. Then she usually makes nests for three or four more groups of eggs.

After five to ten weeks, the eggs hatch. The young salmon are called *alevins*. They stay in the nest and feed on the yolk of the egg they hatched from.

By the time the young salmon leave the nest, they are called *fry*. They have stripes that help them stay hidden from predators. Some kinds of Pacific salmon stay in fresh water for years, but others start migrating to the ocean within a few hours.

On the way to the ocean, the young fish turn silver and become *smolts*. Their new color will help them stay safer on the next part of their journey. As they get close to the ocean, they swim through water that is a mix of fresh water and salt water at the mouth of the river. This place is called an *estuary*. The smolts may stay there for days or months before they enter the ocean.

An *adult* salmon lives in the ocean from six months to seven years. It eats and grows during this time. Many predators—including other fish, seals, sea lions, dolphins, and killer whales—hunt salmon in the ocean.

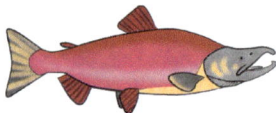

Spawners migrate back to the freshwater stream, river, or lake where they hatched so they can spawn. They stop eating when they reach fresh water. Their body and color change. Most salmon die within a week of when they spawn. After they die, their bodies provide food for many animals and add nutrients to the water.

You're a Salmon!

(continued)

INSTRUCTIONS

1. All players place their markers in the REDD (nest) area.

2. Roll the die to see who goes first. (Then the player on the first player's right will go next.)

3. Player #1 rolls again and moves the correct number of spaces on the board. Then he or she reads aloud any words on that square and follows any instructions. If the player is instructed to move ahead or back, follow the instructions on the new square as well.

4. Then it's Player #2's turn. Players follow the path around the board. The first player to reach the END space in the spawning ground wins.

MATERIALS

- Game board (pages 33–35) taped together

- Markers (such as coins, beans, or markers from another game)

- One die (or a spinner from another game)

ACTIVITY
2

Migration Mapping

INSTRUCTIONS

You've read about many different kinds of animals that migrate. Now it's time to choose one to learn more about! How will you choose an animal? If you want, you can review the animals in the story and choose one of those. If you prefer, you can do your own research (on the Internet or at a library) to find a different animal to learn more about. Here are a few ideas of how to choose your animal:

MATERIALS

- Crayons, markers, or colored pencils
- Yarn or string (optional)
- Glue (optional)

- Type of animal, such as mammal, bird, fish, reptile, amphibian, or insect (For example, type "reptiles that migrate" or "migrating reptiles" in a search engine.)

- Weather patterns (For example, type "coldest animal migrations" in a search engine.)

- Location (For example, type "Australian animal migrations" in a search engine.)

Once you have chosen your animal, read all about it! Find out why it migrates, where it goes, and how it knows where to go. Also find out any other fun facts about your animal. Then fill in your Research Journal (page 41) with all the cool information you discovered!

The art part of this activity is to create a migration map for your chosen animal. Print out a blank map on page 37 (the world) or page 39 (North America) and use any art supplies you'd like to mark the path it travels. You can either draw the path or glue yarn or string on the map. Then decorate the map any way you want. Have fun!

AN EXAMPLE: **Leatherback Sea Turtle Migration Map**

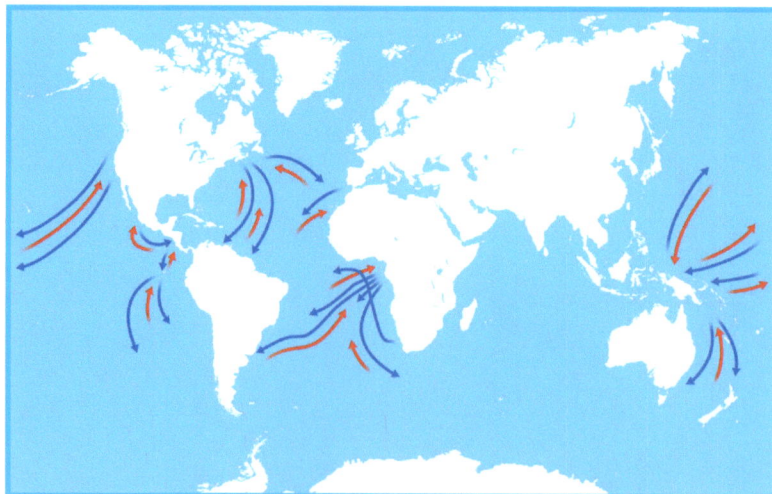

Fly Like a Goose!

Have you ever seen geese flying overhead? If so, you may have noticed that they fly in the shape of the letter V. This arrangement is called a V-formation. Did you ever wonder why geese fly in this way? There are two very good reasons!

First, geese can keep track of each other when they fly in a V. They can see and communicate with each other, which helps keep the flock together.

Second, geese fly in a V-formation because it helps the geese save energy. It takes a lot of energy to be the goose in front because he or she is flying directly into the wind. Because of how air flows, the geese in back of the first one feel less wind when they fly. The geese take turns being in front so everyone works hard for a little while and then gets to rest. Cooperation lightens the load for all the geese. By working together, they can move faster and keep flying much longer than an individual goose could alone. To save energy, they even flap their wings in time with each other!

Would you like to see for yourself how a V-formation works? It's time for you and your friends to be geese!

MATERIALS

- Bath towels (one for each "goose")
- Timer
- Electric fan
- An adult helper

INSTRUCTIONS

1. Gather together an odd-numbered group of friends. Five or seven is perfect, but three will work, too. The diagrams will show the activity for five friends.

2. Each goose holds a towel across his or her shoulders to create a pair of "wings."

3. Choose one friend to be the lead goose. This goose is #1. The other geese each get a number (#2 through #5) and line up behind and to the outside of the lead goose like this:

Step 3

ACTIVITY
3

Fly Like a Goose!

INSTRUCTIONS (continued)

4. The adult helper sets the timer for thirty seconds. (Real geese fly in a certain position for three to four minutes, but that would make this activity take too long.) All the geese practice flying together facing forward. Everyone watches the lead goose and copies his or her movements. They flap their wings at the same speed and lift and lower their wings at the same time.

5. After the timer goes off, it's time to change positions! Start with the back geese on both sides of the V. The back geese change places with geese in front of them. (The lead goose stays in the front for now.)

Step 5

6. The adult helper sets the timer for 30 seconds, and the geese fly in this new arrangement. All eyes are on the lead goose!

7. After the timer goes off, one of the geese changes places with the lead goose so the lead goose gets to rest a little! Goose #5 changes places with the lead goose (#1). Now Goose #5 is the lead goose!

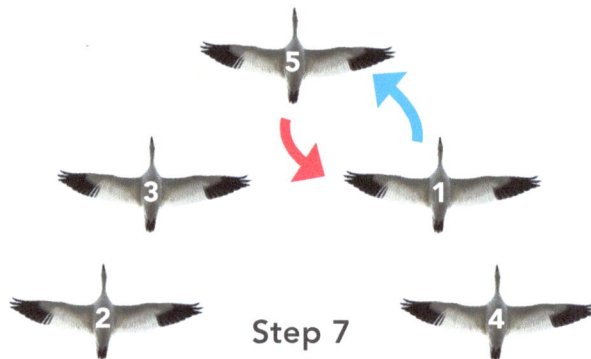

Step 7

ACTIVITY
3

Fly Like a Goose!

INSTRUCTIONS (continued)

8. The adult helper sets the timer for 30 seconds, and the geese fly in this new arrangement. All eyes are on the new lead goose!

9. After the timer goes off, Goose #3 takes over for the new lead goose. Geese #3 and #5 switch positions.

Step 9

10. The adult helper sets the timer for 30 seconds, and the geese fly in this new arrangement. Then the adult asks which geese haven't yet been the lead goose. The group figures out how to change positions so that, one at a time, those geese each take a turn at the front of the flock. When everyone has had a turn as the lead goose, you're ready for the next part of this activity!

11. The adult helper sets up the fan about 8 feet from the lead goose so it blows straight toward the lead goose. Now the flock is flying into the wind, which makes flying harder for real geese. However, the lead goose has the hardest time, while the geese in back are shielded a bit from the force of the wind. The flock flies again (flapping their wings but not moving forward) and notices how much they feel the wind. They can try moving a little bit to the right or left to cut down on the wind.

12. Rotate positions so everyone gets to feel what it's like to be in the front, middle, and back. Then talk about what you noticed.

Fly Like a Goose!

INSTRUCTIONS (continued)

Real geese don't switch positions in exactly the same way as in this activity. Scientists don't actually know the pattern of how geese change positions or how they decide. Bigger geese are likely to prefer the front because they are stronger and like to fly faster. The smaller, weaker geese in back have an easier time because they have more protection from the wind.

The next time you're outside and see geese flying overhead, notice how they line up in a V-formation. Watch to see if any of them change positions. Think about how well geese work together to help the whole flock have an easier journey.

ACTIVITY
4

Tracking Monarchs

You learned a little about monarch butterflies in the Migration Awards story. You may already know something about their life cycle, so here's just a quick review:

An adult female monarch lays eggs on a milkweed plant.

Larvae (LAR-vee), or caterpillars, hatch from the eggs. They eat the milkweed plant and grow, grow, grow! They molt, or shed their skin four or more times as they get bigger. A caterpillar is full grown after about two weeks. Then it makes silk and attaches itself to a leaf or stem.

During the pupa, or chrysalis, stage, the insect is changing from a caterpillar into a butterfly inside a case. This process is called metamorphosis. It lasts about ten days.

An adult butterfly emerges after the process is complete. At first, its wings are soft and folded. After three or four hours, the butterfly will be able to fly. It will fly off to find nectar to drink.

Tracking Monarchs

ACTIVITY 4

(continued)

Here's some more information about monarchs:

COOL FACTS ABOUT MONARCH BUTTERFLIES

- Know how to tell male and female monarchs apart? Behind each male's hind wing is a black spot that females don't have. Also, females often have wider veins on their wings than males.

- Monarch butterflies migrate—but not all of them! Four generations, or age groups, of monarchs emerge each year from their chrysalis. The first three groups die after about six weeks. Only the fourth group will migrate.

- Some monarchs live in warm enough places that they have everything they need all year. They don't migrate, either!

- Monarch butterflies come from North and South America. In the 1800s, they spread to Hawaii and the South Pacific Ocean around Australia.

- Monarchs use the sun, mountains, and bodies of water to help them find their way when they migrate. Air currents help them stay on track. Forest smells may help them know they're close to the end of their journey.

- When monarchs arrive in their winter location, they hibernate in large groups. So many of them may rest on the same tree branch that their weight breaks the branch!

What are you CURIOUS about?

ACTIVITY
4

Tracking Monarchs

(continued)

Do you live in an area with monarch butterflies? If so, do you know what time of the year they are there? Check out this map to find out the general areas where monarchs are found:

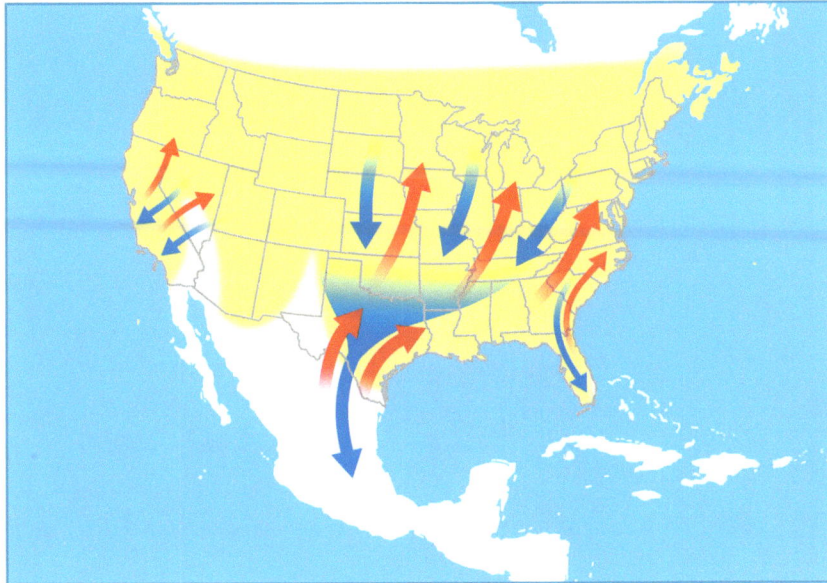

Would you like to watch for monarch butterflies? You can be part of a citizen science project! Visit the Monarch Butterfly Journey North website here: http://www.learner.org/jnorth/monarch/

Click on the "Kids" link to find all sorts of amazing resources on monarch butterflies (including cool time-lapse photos!) From the main "Kids" page, click on "Citizen Science" to learn about helping scientists track monarchs.

Now return to the homepage and click on "Sightings" at the top. If you see a monarch, you can register as a new user and report your sighting! You can also view other people's sightings from the current season or past seasons.

ACTIVITY
4

Tracking Monarchs

(continued)

What to report:

- First monarch in spring, along with wind, weather, and habitat conditions

- First milkweed

- First monarch egg

- First monarch larva

Be sure to also fill in your Field Journal (page 43) with information about your sighting!

FOR EXTRA FUN:

The same "Sightings" page has a dropdown menu where you can report sightings of MANY other animals, including gray whales, bats, eagles, and hummingbirds. The same menu also lists other signs of spring you can report.

Would you like to learn about or participate in other citizen science projects? Type the name of a migrating animal and "citizen science" OR "report sighting" in your favorite search engine, and see what you come up with! Here are a few to get you started:

Hummingbirds: http://www.hummingbirds.net/index.html

Frogs and toads: https://www.aza.org/frogwatch/

Fireflies: https://legacy.mos.org/fireflywatch/

A variety of birds: http://www.ebird.org/content/ebird/about/

Backyard birds: http://gbbc.birdcount.org/

Curiosity Connector

Here are some links to help you follow your curiosity!

- Read more about migrating animals here:
  http://www.kidsdiscover.com/spotlight/animal-migrations-for-kids/

- See amazing photos of migrating animals here:
  http://www.huffingtonpost.com/2014/04/02/animal-migrations_n_4941847.html

- Watch some cool video clips about migrating animals here:
  http://www.watchknowlearn.org/Category.aspx?CategoryID=6727

- Learn more about monarch butterflies here:
  http://www.monarch-butterfly.com/monarch-butterflies-facts.html

- Enjoy a video clip of Jeff Corwin with monarch butterflies:
  http://www.youtube.com/watch?v=tFT7BfN69s0

- See a list of many of the animals that migrate here:
  http://www.thefreeresource.com/migration-what-is-migration-list-of-animals-that-migrate-and-fun-facts
  Use the list to follow your curiosity and read about migrating animals you don't already know about!

What are you CURIOUS about?

Glossary

BREEDING GROUNDS – a natural area where a group of animals regularly go to mate, lay eggs or give birth, and raise their young

CITIZEN SCIENCE – collecting and studying information about the natural world by members of the general public, usually as part of a project run by scientists

FEEDING GROUNDS – a natural area where a group of animals go to look for food and eat it

HIBERNATE – to go into a state of rest or deep sleep, often during winter

LANDMARKS – easily seen objects on land that can be used to find one's way

MAGNETIC FIELD – an area around Earth or another object where there is a magnetic force, which pushes and pulls certain metals

MIGRATION – a pattern of movement from one location to another that a certain animal follows, usually more than once a year

PREDATORS – animals that hunt and eat other animals for food

SHELTER – a place that offers protection from bad weather or danger

SIGHTINGS – acts of seeing something for a short period of time, especially something unusual

SPAWNING GROUNDS – a natural area where a group of fish or certain other types of animals go to lay eggs in water

TEMPERATE – located in a part of the world that is midway between the equator and the poles and usually has mild temperatures

TROPICAL – located in a part of the world that is close to the equator and usually has hot, humid weather

Tools for Your Tool Kit

Let's make the ideas you learned today part of your life tool kit. Remember to print out some blank tool kit pages and tape or glue on today's tools.

1. The places where salmon go to lay eggs are their _____ .

   Add **SPAWNING GROUNDS** to your tool kit!

2. The places where animals travel to find food are their _____ .

   Add **FEEDING GROUNDS** to your tool kit!

3. The places where animals travel to mate and raise their young are their _____

   _____ .

   Add **BREEDING GROUNDS** to your tool kit!

4. _____ involves moving from one place to another, usually more than once in the same year.

   Add **MIGRATION** to your tool kit!

5. When you visit a special website to report seeing monarch butterfies in a certain place on a certain date, you are reporting your _____ .

   Add **SIGHTINGS** to your tool kit!

Cutout for Activity 1: You're a Salmon!

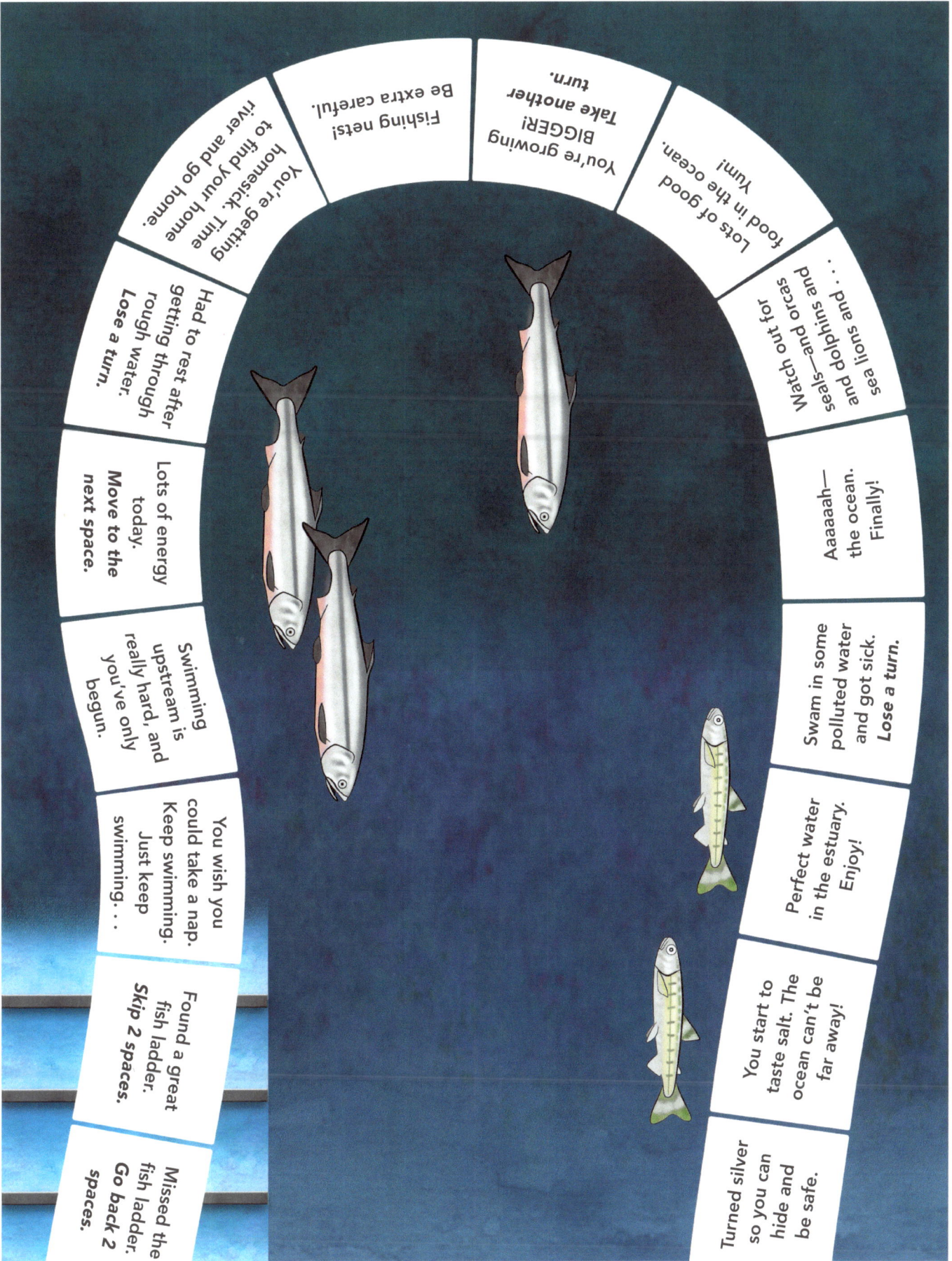

You're getting homesick. Time to find your home river and go home.

Fishing nets! Be extra careful.

You're growing BIGGER! Take another turn.

Lots of good food in the ocean. Yum!

Had to rest after getting through rough water. **Lose a turn.**

Lots of energy today. **Move to the next space.**

Swimming upstream is really hard, and you've only begun.

You wish you could take a nap. Keep swimming. Just keep swimming...

Found a great fish ladder. **Skip 2 spaces.**

Missed the fish ladder. **Go back 2 spaces.**

Turned silver so you can hide and be safe.

You start to taste salt. The ocean can't be far away!

Perfect water in the estuary. Enjoy!

Swam in some polluted water and got sick. **Lose a turn.**

Aaaaaah— the ocean. Finally!

Watch out for seals—and orcas and dolphins and ... and sea lions and ...

The water is too warm today. Just keep swimming. . .

The river is sluggish today. **Lose a turn.**

Got stripes on your body. Woo-hoo!

The water is too warm today. Hang in there!

Your yummy yolk sac gave you lots of energy. **Move ahead 1 space.**

What a great place! Remember where it is so you can come back.

REDD Got a great start in cool, clear water! **Move ahead 1 space.**

GO THIS WAY

END Your work is done. You've had a good life full of amazing adventures.

You remember this place! Time to lay some eggs and make more of your kind.

CONGRATS! You made it home! Great job!

You couldn't possibly be more tired. Luckily, you're almost home.

What a hard trip! But something is calling you home, and you can't stop.

That bear didn't notice you. You're safe for now!

Lost one of your buddies to the bear, but there's no time to stop and feel sad.

Yikes! A bear!

Migration Map for

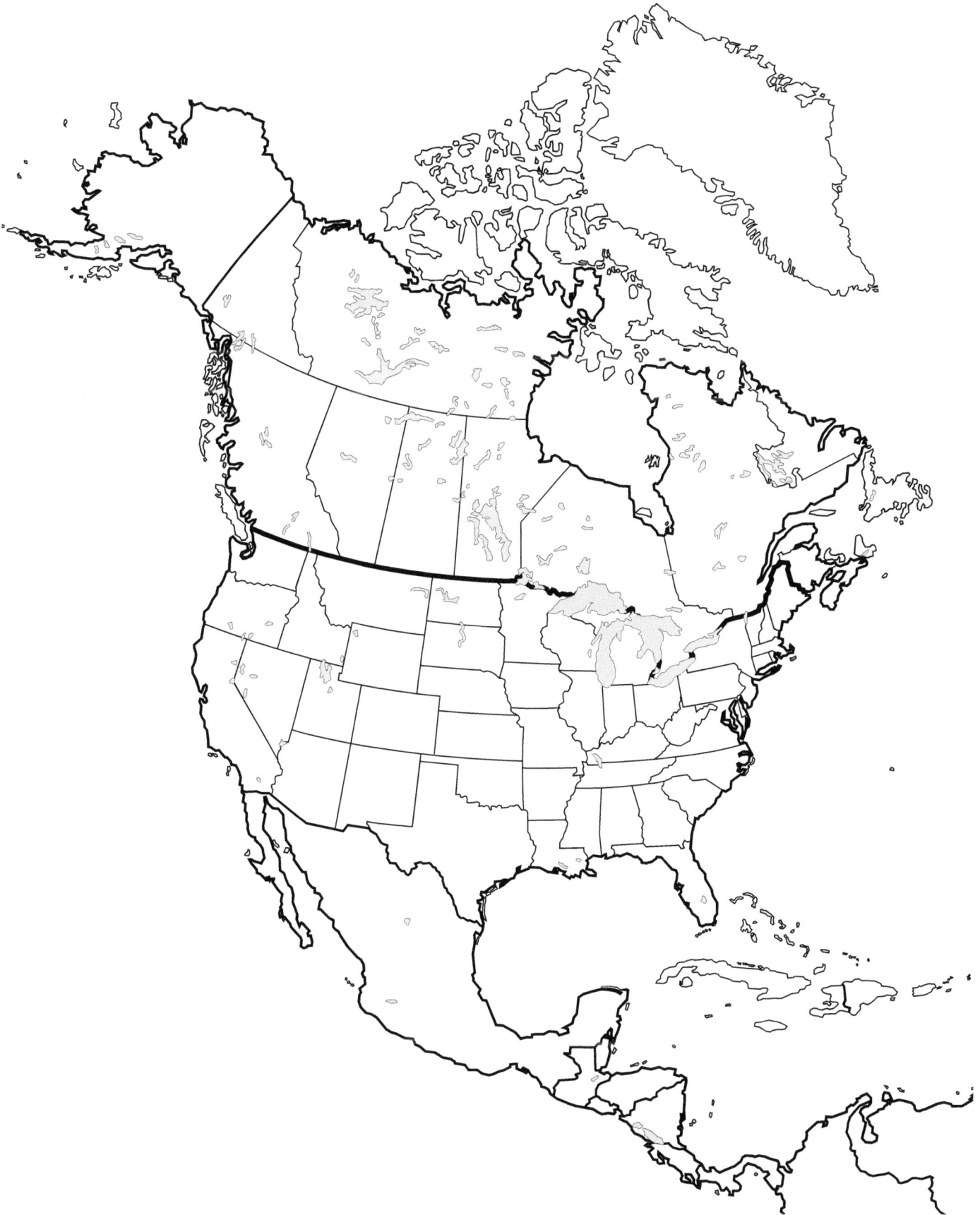

Migration Map for _____

ACTIVITY 2

Research Journal

Type of animal (mammal, bird, etc.):

_____

Where it migrates from:

_____

Where it migrates to:

_____

Time of year it migrates:

_____

Draw a picture of your migrating animal:

Purpose(s) of migration (see pg. 4): _____

Eats along the way? _____

Rests along the way? _____

Dangers during migration: _____

Other fascinating facts about this animal's migration: _____

_____

_____

Other fascinating general information about this animal: _____

_____

_____

BONUS: Changes in your animal's migration route or conditions over time: _____

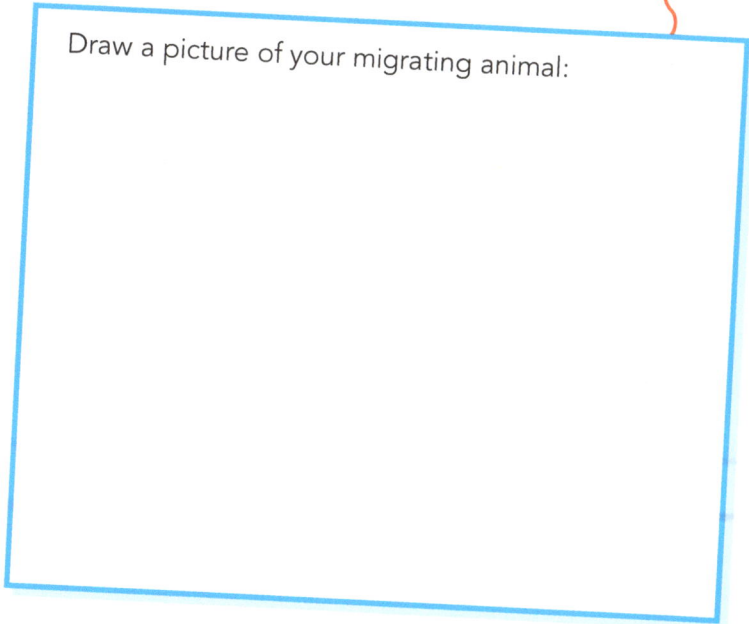

_____

_____

Cutout for Activity 2: Migration Mapping

ACTIVITY 4

Field Journal

Did you see (circle one):   a monarch butterfly?   a caterpillar?   a pupa?

Draw a picture of what you saw in the left-hand box.
If you took a photo, print it out and tape or glue it in the right-hand box.

Observations

Where did you see the monarch? _____

Was it flying or sitting on something? _____

Was it eating? _____

What was the environment in which you found it (woods, fields, etc.)? _____

_____

_____

What time of year did you see it? _____

What time of day did you see it? _____

Did you see a milkweed plant nearby? _____

Science Tool Kit

www.ingramcontent.com/pod-product-compliance
Lightning Source LLC
LaVergne TN
LVHW072130070426
835513LV00002B/49